IN THE EYE OF THE RED-TAILED HAWK: AN ESSAY ON LOVE

Don Washburn

THE POET'S PRESS
Providence, RI

Copyright © 2009 by Don Washburn

ISBN 0-922558-40-X

This is the 181st book published by
THE POET'S PRESS
279-1/2 Thayer Street
Providence, RI 02906

Also published as an e-book
in Adobe Acrobat Format

www.poetspress.org

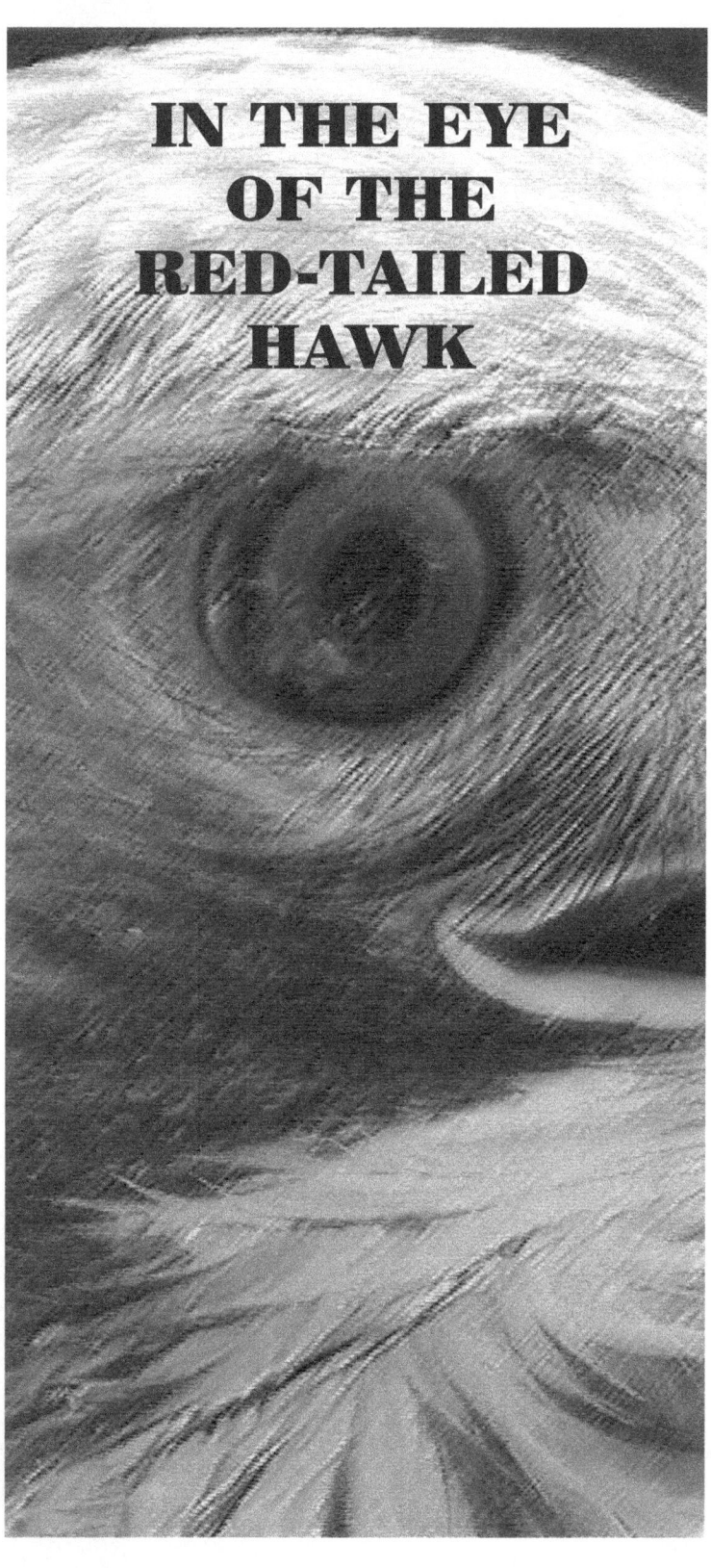

IN THE EYE OF THE RED-TAILED HAWK

1
GETTING TOGETHER

The world opens, through the tiniest pin-pricks,
through obscure wormholes, through narrow
    spotlights,
scattering the dark. Then the enormous matrix
of separation parts like a curtain. The stage lights
up. And you are present. But why just you
out of the myriads. And why just now? Why this
concatenation of events that brought us to
mix our several substances in a kiss?
Is there a greater plan perhaps? Assignations?
Shadowy figures in the wings, who wait and come
in their own time, each bearing libations
from on high. Each a dispensation from
the Source of All. How many are lingering
    and might
draw near — but only as the light grows bright?

2
THE STARSHIP

Or maybe I am a starship, circling an unknown
world. Your face, a mystery. Your secret mind,
a colony. Think what earth births, all overgrown
with the profligate prodigies of animal kind.
What forms can take shape in an alien wilderness?
What dragons lurk there, breathing fire?
      What mermaids
tangle the senses? What shadowy abysses
lie in wait? What predators ply their trades?
When our eyes lock, sometimes I feel
in that stare a certain ruthlessness. An arctic
terrain inhospitable to love. But I appeal
the evidence of instruments. They are too quick.
Captains must see for themselves. Scotty, beam
me down! And keep me safe if I dream.

3
FINGERS

Touch is a language. And though my house is dark,
I feel the light. I am myself a lamp here.
The Lord of Harmony is never far.
He has His luminous fingers in my hair.
My kingdom is restored, but only the ambient
bunny thumps at night under the recliner
to have her muzzle stroked. When I assent,
my solitary moments grow kinder.
She has scheduled this time for her caresses.
Her simple heart makes a meadow of me.
When I stroke her ears, she acquiesces.
Thus do we make a willing couple. Her silky
fur needs petting, fits me like a glove,
and at least my fingers keep the habit of love.

4
THE MOOSE

Your e-mail handle was "the traveling moose."
I saw a moose in Maine one time on TV. A man
came out of a store. It kicked him to death. Who's
going to mess with something like that? I can,
I thought. When my guides embrace me at the end,
I want no reproach for being self-absorbed,
too timid, too much alone. No, I don't intend
to live in fear, the lion in me roared.
Ride the untamable moose. Perform your stunts
with hat in hand, my bucko. Do not take less
than the terror and joy at the crux of things. Once
you turned and said with a certain ruefulness,
"I see I have not scared you off." Good guess.
Not even a chance, I answered under my breath.

5
WATERS

Angels envy us the waters. The blood's tides
and the wash of senses. The tsunami of passion
that wrecks our shores. These will be our guides:
The star who has a double and looks to fashion
herself like a starfish in the cove. The dolphin
who lifts to gulp the air but takes delight
in the surge of the surf. The gull who skims in
playful waters, another kind of flight.
Cherish spirit, but the body too will teach,
where the watery blood burns like a sun.
Let us dive and be submerged, each
in the other, becoming for a moment one.
Grow wings we must. But grow also fins,
to swim in love's seas, our bright origins.

6
GLASS WALLS

Have you seen the angels come down, wielding
their fiery sledge-hammers? Have you heard them
    shattering
the glass walls where limits live? Those now
    are yielding.
Sometimes the angels pause to scold, nattering:
"Do the most exquisite blooms grow
    in a greenhouse?
Fool! Do you really think you can keep the divine
ishk at bay? Let the wind of the spirit move
    and arouse
you! Open your breath. Be God's libertine.
By hiding beneath, just who are you saving?
An old man creeps to his death-bed
    not having lived.
But when these panes shatter, he's out-braving
demise, and takes with his passing a joyful gift.
Be stalwart then! Better to ride, perforce,
a wild moose than suffocate indoors."

7
FIRST DATE

OK, don't call it a date. Say I just happened
to pull into the parking lot. And there you were.
Enough of patriarchy and the vapid
conventionalities that compromise allure.
Call it an accident, an act of God, a freak of nature.
Make it as unofficial as you like. And if I pick up
the check, stop me, make it something you're
doing yourself, as impersonal as this cup.
Maybe it is just "hanging out," something
that could easily dissolve and float away.
There are no meanings here. Just the ping
of dishes in the kitchen. Just another day.
Have it any way you want. My eyes look straight
to where yours look. With them I am having a date.

8
THE CEMETERY POND

The pond on one side, the falls on the other,
we straddle the bench and are connected.
The pond, for all its peace, contains another
sky, where hemlocks rise, perfectly reflected.
And beneath, a tadpole heaven is teeming with life.
The falls, opposite, dazzles with its streamings
And takes us below where the runnings writhe,
making frothy rapids of all our meanings.
Our eyes dart between this world and that
to find an oracle, to welcome or refuse,
seeking in this earnest speech the caveat
that blots a future or sanctions what we choose.
The water is moving, but we move too,
and change with our intentions what we do.

9
THE STONE ANGEL

It seems we've been summoned to this spot, where
the white angel spreads her marble wings,
stone intricate as feathers. We pause here
awhile, in her shadow, listening to things
half-heard, gathering strange knowledge — you
who love omens and I, haunter of cemeteries.
The silence takes us in. Walking through
death's kingdom, we search out harmonies.
At the angel's feet we sit a moment, call forth
a blessing on our enterprise. For this
commands our best. And may the sweet earth
and this day's sky be our loving witness.
How can we not humble ourselves, gazing above,
and find in this icon the doorway to our love?

10

MARY AND EBENEZER

We asked permission before we sat down, side
by side, on your gravestones, a handy place
on our jaunt. I smiled to think the dead invite
such wanderers in to their parlor space.
Were you happy to hold us for a moment, as you
once held one another? Lovers, no doubt, come
seldom to your resting place. That you were true
we trust, coveting ourselves this premium.
Now you are privy to our reverie
if words can pass through veils and transcend.
Maybe we caused a stir in your ghostly
bosoms and reminded you there is no end
to this immortal dance that we've just started,
though you are silent now and long departed.

11
THE BLUSH

Since you are the professor of blushes and read
mine with such confidence, can you live
with what you publish? Isn't your thesis your need:
outlining such pleasure as my fingers give,
or my tongue, making ripples on your breast,
or our lips meeting ever so sensuously?
If you would expose in me the Freudian beast,
does not your own mind mount the satyr to be
ravished? To this text surely you bring
great scholarship. Study and broad research
seasons judgment. But if these imputations ring
true, there is between us some untold urge.
My face is a book containing your coy intent.
Who then is bawdy and who is innocent?

12
PERSONAL HISTORY

God knows we've both been around the block
and stood in many lines. The old movies keep
cranking. When you spin your tales, the clock
stops. I need to concentrate and take a deep
breath. I listen as though my life depended
on it. Your ancient mariner's eyes skewer me.
The plots thicken. You tell me how you fended
off one disaster after another.
      Prisoner of catastrophe,
your life unfolds just this side of death.
Could be the astonished Caliph was heard to say —
when Scheherazade paused to catch her breath —
"I've hearkened to a lot of yarn-meisters in my day,
hawking calamities and close calls too.
One more won't matter if she's as plucky as you."

13
GRAVITY

This is what I would say to you if it could be
said. Love is the world's fifth force and the greatest.
It draws together by some dark mystery
one soul and another. In that free fall best
to abandon safety. Best to give up all fear,
overturning even reason itself. For the sweet
gravity is its own argument. And the clear
energies will wash away pain. Every defeat
is reversed in the instant the heart is truly given.
Who does not live for that balm? What is more
wholesome and holy? Though the flesh be riven
and expectations torn, this is the hope we live for.
Let us honor, then, whatever it is we feel,
for by this medicine we truly heal.

14

WILD FLOWERS

My love had a busy day, selling off her goods,
chatting with neighbors. And the visitors
     kept coming.
In this tag sale there were no interludes.
The front door grew dizzy with all that drumming.
One friend gave the knob into the hand of another.
All day welcoming people, talking for hours,
she finally had to take her leave just to recover.
And on her walk she found the wild flowers,
made a fragrant bouquet, and brought them home.
What more could you possibly want in this poem?

15
TAG SALE

While you are having your tag sale, why not do
it right? Sell off the defenses, all the doubts
and fears. Search the inside-yourself rooms too.
Bag and curb your "what-ifs." Don't be too proud.
Discard the scary stories: the betrayals, the lies,
the degradations, the scenes of shame, the dark
rain of soullessness, the faces and cruel eyes
of those who used you, the crimes against the heart.
How can you stand in the clear light with so
much clutter? How can you see me with eyes
haunted by phantoms? Take a broom and go
chase them out. Clean house. Nobody buys
such sorry leftovers, so out the door!
Pile them off to the dumpster. Really start over.

16
STIRRING BEANS

Some think that love is a pot of beans, sitting
on the stove. All day under a low flame
the beans soften and grow fit for eating.
The hourglass empties grain by grain.
But I think it is a flash from the unseen world —
an instant recognition. It is the warp
of gravity that bends the light. It is the whirled
trajectory of an angel's sword.
It is the moment the imagination turns
and declares itself. "I could fall in love
with you," I said too soon. But a fire burns
where there is fuel. And a circling dove
finds a perch. I am already there it seems.
But until you catch up, I'll pretend
      I am stirring beans.

17
THE BUTTERFLY

Sometimes I catch the meaning of things. Take
the butterfly you wore on your belt, ablaze
with sequins and colors of the sun. I make
it out a symbol of the soul and the ways
our larval selves become something beautiful.
That quote you asked me about — Murshid saying
how the purpose of life is to attain the jewel
of mastery, what light desires in its playing.
Is it not the perfection of love! Perhaps
this is why we are here. But all will come
to nothing if we cannot rise above mishaps
and find our meaning in the spirit's curriculum.
Let us learn from the butterfly and so aspire:
first the soul — then the heart — then desire.

18

CHOCOLATE MOUSSE

My weakness for chocolate mousse
      has become my weakness
for the "traveling moose," she who collects
      speeding tickets
and counts the moose statues in Bennington.
      And this
dish of chocolate mousse she's brought me — its
flavor lasts weeks. My pun on moose had her
for its object. She is the mousse I savor. I blurt
this without even blushing. My tongue
      would rather
sample her, since she is the more delicious dessert.
As my senses luxuriate in the dark sweetness,
I think, what good is a life without pleasure?
The goddess wills beauty — stirs us with this —
and worlds have been confected beyond measure.
I know where my sweet tooth will have its fix:
she is the delightful bowl where sugars mix.

19

E-MAIL

All these servants waiting on our love!
In the morning the genie of electricity
carries our greetings to start the day. Above
the keyboard a silicon orchestra plays
the libretto that gets us to sleep. Our words
are tumbled in the lap of processors more
clever than imps. Like a flight of birds,
our weightiest thoughts take wing and soar.
We hang a hundred dates in that Web.
It dangles our flirtations on the screen,
just a finger's length away from instant gab.
We saddle this pander, this speedy go-between,
with welcome tidings, confidences that might
serve affection's most exacting appetite.

20
THE WHITE ROSE

To celebrate our single summer of grace,
you clipped a white rose while you walked
and put it on the table in a vase.
There it sat between us while we talked.
Together we gazed out through the glass doors
into the arbor, watching the play of light,
dreaming of realities unseen. In our metaphors
we found another way to school our sight.
And for the moment made perfect company,
conjecturing imponderables, a play of mind
which like a blossom has its time to be.
In such a way all beauty is divined.
Petals have a shape that rinses the sight
and the soul is in love with the color white.

21
THE TAVERN

Your story about the tavern: how heart-sore
with loneliness you found a watering hole near —
only three streets over. You went in the door
to a world of sweat, darkness, and stale beer.
Only to see a patron and his woman
at the bar, his hand stroking her behind,
as though the invisible ones had brought you in
to see more clearly what you would surely find.
Not then the honky-tonk girl of days long past,
you felt a certain stirring of the light.
"Is this what you want?" an inner voice asked.
The exit was your answer. And so good-night.
I felt your victory, raised from that catacomb.
Refusing the lesser is half of what brings us home.

22
HAREM

What you called my "harem" was my curriculum.
I learned by rote the hazards of the heart.
She turned fire to ice. She loved anyone.
She longed to lie with women. She slept apart.
She was a money pit. She dated death.
She used me for a fool. She fondled me and left.
She taught waiting. She taught touch and breath.
Each came in time and with a precious gift.
She taught me constancy. She taught me peace.
The briar of bitterness, I watered with my tears.
The very life that shattered signed another lease.
And taking heart, I overcame my fears.
Embrace this rich history then. It is my tenderness,
my hard-won schooling. Would you have me less?

23
PRAYER TO PRIAPUS

I humble myself, old friend, and hie
to apologize for cutting you off so brusquely
in my monkish solitude. I confess I
thought you a nuisance, even in your divinity,
and surely gave offense. Yet lately
I've revived and become more enterprising.
Now I ask forgiveness, if only for my lady's
sake, whose delight is fitted to your rising.
If you must punish, be merciful. No stud
am I now in my ripeness, commanding those same
energies that once made a carnival of my blood.
I am grey, but have been your servant
      and will remain.
Grant me your favor then if you deem it just,
that I may pour desire in my lady's cup.

24

SPADEWORK

Those days when you were putting your garden
    to rest
for the winter, when you were digging
    into the ground
and turning it over, when your hands were stressed
and raw from the heft of the shovel, perhaps
    you found
your mind was also doing some digging into
the soil that shaped you, unearthing the sour
roots of pain, exhuming the gritty slew
of decay that had its ineluctable hour.
Air and light will make themselves your pardoner.
The excavations of this husbandry search
to make all things healthy. My sweet gardener,
use me, if you wish, like some comforting mulch,
like some healing compost, reanimating
the crops and blooms of your approaching spring.

25
FACING

Caught up in your gaze, that unflinching look,
that I can only compare to the eyes of the hawks
I saw at The Bird Paradise, I am an open book.
I become transparent. In these talks
we have, I live in total exposure to what
will seize me. If sometimes I seem in awe
and cannot hide my thoughts, I've got
my charter, knowing only heaven's law —
there can be no lies between us, no art.
So I can say without embarrassment
your face is written in light across my heart
just below God's name. Even the dissent
lurking in your impish grin is in accord
with the prophet's paradise and virtue's reward.

26
BLOWING ON COALS

After fifty, sex is like blowing on coals.
Our forgetful bodies want the heat of passion.
Only love, the great aphrodisiac, enthralls,
enlivens all seven chakras, turns ashen
lips incarnadine, and repeals
the floe of lassitude that cools our blood.
Then our Indian Summer arrives, feels
this warmth out of season. The untimely bud
of passion quickens like a match. And our hot
breath feathers the kindled flesh. Like seasoned
wood we wait for deepest burning. Is this not
good husbandry and the sweetest reason,
that frees the logjam of our lustful art
until a cheery fire is burning on the hearth?

27
THE L-WORD

You said you did not know what love is.
A burst of sunlight on a dark day, I thought.
And if I said the L-word first, paralysis
kept you silent. But one night you caught
me by surprise. I heard it clearly like
a bell ringing. I felt it up and down
my spine. Such simple syllables can strike
a blow for rapture, turn everything around.
Now we can move together with a single
beat, I thought. And speak our hearts without
restraint. And when we walk together, mingle
with all those who no longer doubt,
joining, like two arriving fashionably
late, love's open and festive company."

28

MIGRATING GEESE

Over the field where we ran the Shelties
that day, the wild geese came flying down
low, scribbling the October sky with endless V's
and filling the air with their haunting,
      honking sound.
Wave after wave, they came by —
      in the hundreds — while
astonished, we gaped at the wonder of so much
direction, so much life and certainty.
      Whatever guile
ordered their course, their flying
      was as sure as touch.
And reminded us of the truth of all journeys,
that love itself has its compass, and when
it hazards the unknown, may think on these.
Even left behind, we cast our eyes after them —
and followed with migratory spirits of our own,
wild with thinking how much is waiting
      to be known.

29
THE PIR'S POD

The day we climbed into the woods to the Pir's
pod, the domed Quonset where he did his work,
we put aside our egos and our fears,
to find the retreat of our vanished patriarch.
Arriving, we chatted briefly, but grew still.
The jingling wind chimes composed
      a haunting music.
The leaves were bright with sunlight on that hill.
We heard the endless water rushing in the creek.
Inside, we sat in meditation. Here
was the chair he sat in, and here was his bowl.
What did we hope to find together? A clear
moment, a radiance to make us whole.
We still carry with us that ambience
and know of a silence that is more than silence.

30

DINING

In the heart's five-star restaurant, I loved to
watch you cook, whipping up meals fit
for a king. Poised at the stove, meticulous, you,
danced pans in your hands. It was an exquisite
ballet — a study in exactitude and grace.
The food obeyed you and found a shape
that pleased an artist's eye. And at such a pace
I could only marvel, could only gape.
What discipline, I saw, what practiced intent.
You were a genie, the stomach's favorite.
The very spices clapped their astonishment!
And my mouth waters just to think of it.
The dishes were served. Delightful the smell.
And not even that other Jamshyd ate so well.

31
THE PENDULUM

You are my lady of synchronicities.
An oracle sits on your hip, as rhythmic as
a heartbeat. When you go to your pocket and tease
it out — yes — or no — or maybe — it says.
This swinging coin is a choice coin of the realm,
a withdrawal from that invisible bank where
fortunes beckon. Watchful at this small helm,
you blithely chart your course without a care.
Thus do you place your intentions at auction,
and I do your bidding. By such faith, arousing
my own sense of servitude, I take instruction,
bending my wishes to its artful dowsing.
If you need to fathom why I am so bent,
know this: I am in your life with its consent.

32
THE IRON HORSE

My love gave me an iron horse to set over
my fireplace. Iron against iron, she said,
is needed to sharpen things. I have seen her
file the kitchen knives to a perfect edge.
The man she'd married saddled horses up.
They were his darlings. (That was one complaint.)
I see him with the harness, the bridle, the crop,
the reins, a veritable lasso of constraint.
But what do I know of leather or the will
to subdue intractable things? I cannot be
a creature of iron and earth. Rather I thrill
to wind that sweeps the prairie and is free.
There the herds run wild, their eyes on fire,
and I hear only the hoof beats of desire.

33
THE GARGOYLE

Lovecraft would have seen it immediately.
But when you pointed it out to me, "Over there,
on the grey house . . ." I was aghast. Mocking me,
high in the eaves, fronting the street, the stare
of pure evil for all to see, carved in wood,
the hideous grimace of malevolence, raised high,
a painted emblem of the house. I could
feel the weight of that leaden sky.
From what deep wounds comes this ferocity?
What does this omen speak? Your face, a mask,
offered no clue. The veiled world silently
turned away. And so I did not ask,
but inwardly felt how this menace
      darkened our day.
Quickening the pace, we hurried on our way.

34
THE YELLOW CAT

I have nothing in common with the yellow cat
that bit your wrist. Showing me your town,
you bent to stroke the creature where it sat
and went too far. The wrist still hurts down
deep, where the flesh it seems remembers things.
And those other hurts throb too, the ones we
suffer to be ourselves. And even growing wings
will not blot out our scars or history.
But do not withhold your touch, I beg. Cats of
this world are there to be stroked. Better to ache
than be constrained. Better to live with love
than cowardice. Surely the passions
      are there to slake.
Besides, no violence hides under my fur.
When you are close, my dear, I only purr.

35
CRACKS

On windshields, you said, a tiny crack, that seems
nothing at first, can inescapably crawl
and slowly work its way, until the seams,
finally fissure and break, shattering all.
Is this not like the pain which lovers feel
at betrayal or cruelty, or words spoken
in anger? Things that no apologies heal.
Trust fractures this way when trust is broken.
Let us drive carefully then and beseech
our officers to protect us on back roads
and from the daredevils within, that screech
tires, kicking up pebbles. For the sign that slows
us will keep our breakable hearts from hurt,
so long as we are honest and alert.

36
TRUST

When the heart is given, a dagger points
to that tender home, a dagger in your hand.
Do not grow careless, beloved. This giving appoints
you mother to my pulse and the grand
safe-keeper of my pain. A simple sign
draws blood and is hostage to your smile.
Mercy then must be your study. And mine.
Yet, I have a shield which saves me all the while
and sets you free. For I have become fierce
in injury and make it my medicine,
concocting wholeness of whatever appears
in the house of incidents I wander in.
Your kindness then is the substance of my trust,
but if it must, let the dagger thrust.

37
SILVER LAKE

The day we went looking for Silver Lake
the long trail took us off the mark. Eager
for some vantage point, we turned to make
a shortcut up the ridge. We scanned the meager
vistas only to find ourselves looking back
from where we'd come, at another lake
spread out below. So too, do we backtrack
in the wilderness our sad histories make.
And those who trek together and hope to be
lovers may lose the direction and the height.
Silver Lake waits there still, patiently,
its ghostly waters filling up with light,
but we could not find our way.
      Though most contrive
to finish every journey — not all arrive.

38
TOKENS

Circling and circling, always the red-tailed hawk,
that totem, that alter ego, patrolling your skies,
whose shrill cry you mingled with your own talk,
who lived in the crosshairs of your merciless eyes.
And the python that wrapped itself
      around your arm —
you thrilled to the awful power of that embrace,
found in the ravenous coiling no cause for alarm,
as though the cold blood ran in your own face.
And the Venus flytrap — how did you feel
when the bee blundered into its sticky maw?
You had no qualm, thought only of the meal,
as though compassion was not another law.
How then do I find my way? These tokens say
you are the predator. And am I then the prey?

39
ATLANTIC CROSSING

I think of you flying high above the dark Atlantic,
all night the drone of jet engines in your ear,
returning to your origins. Arithmetic
makes all crossings precarious, but I do not fear
what angels have labored to provide. My mind
is a postcard with snowy mountains and Swiss
lakes. I am barely visible in the photo. You'll find
me in the amulet circling your neck. That is
as dear as the message on the card you sent:
"I am never far from you, since I carry you
in my heart wherever I go." Since you went,
I watch the calendar as the days accrue.
And I feel the miracle of things, a miracle which is
fearless in the face of darkness and distances.

40
WIND

How many times did you type, "I send
my love on the wind." Now with your
      December trip
half over and the dark mornings starting to end,
I am a prisoner in expectation's grip
and live in the trackless snowfall of this page.
Counting the days, I listen for the wind
and grow soulful. My mind has become a stage
on which your absence plays its violin.
Can continents rob us of our voices and contrive
so much silence after so much talk? The birds,
too, are quiet now. Yet my mind is alive
with conversations: I am saving all my words.
They will blizzard in our joyful atmospheres
when we embrace. And the wind will howl
      in our ears.

41
THE CROWS

No paper out here for me, nor Santa Claus.
But your friends the crows salute me. Two days ago
I saw a hundred fly by. Their shrill caws were cause
enough to pause. If I could sound out just so —
the way you do sometimes, talking to the sky,
I would make a speech in crow language, and say
how on this cold Christmas morning I
hold you in my thoughts. And how today
the only present I need is the certainty you
exist. And so I pause here in my robe
and send you greetings with this dark crew.
Can crow-talk go half way around the globe,
to where you are opening who knows what fine
gifts? No matter. I am content with mine.

42

ASTRAL-GRAM

On the longest night, just before the solstice,
half way through your trip,
      did you send me a dream?
I knew from the fierce locking of our eyes that this
woman was you. Funny how things can seem.
Scene 1: The character playing you was a soloist,
but she could not fit her own song to the piece.
The ensemble was not working. She missed beats.
She botched the complex harmonies.
Scene 2: In a book I kept my spiritual lessons,
writing them down as I am writing this.
I imagined you had arrived at a truer essence.
I thought you'd outfaced your old nemesis,
keeping time with a new beat and with me. Yet,
is this the astral-gram I was meant to get?

43

DECEMBER

The two wings of spirituality, Murshid says,
are detachment and independence.
     But the December weeks,
wordless with you away, are a gaping abyss,
where, like Alaskan nights, a slow procession
     creeps.
I pretend I am strong enough to be without the sun
and nobly declare, I know it is all for the best.
I know you need to do this. But anyone can see
my bravado is futile and a frosty jest.
To keep warm, I strike memories like flint.
Even your photo scatters heat. But these
are only sparks. Where's the supernova to print
on my senses fiery and palpable guarantees?
These hands, like some desperate midwife,
want to grasp you in the flesh, hold on for dear life.

44
BUS STOP

Strange that day I waited for the bus,
all packed to bring you home again. My mind
flew with you across the sea. I thought of us
and how long absences can be unkind.
But your arrival filled my inner eye;
the joy the heart can feel my heart felt.
One by one the others filed by.
The driver had not seen you, could not help.
And then the fear you might have come to harm,
frantic inquiries, an eternity on the phone,
relief that you had landed, but alarm
that you'd checked out, whereabouts unknown.
How could I see the bus was just a sign?
Something had stopped and at the end of the line.

45
RESCUE

Love sometimes proves herself a wavering spirit,
a watery rainbow in the rushing brook,
music so subdued that none can hear it,
grave-flowers dying while the mourners look.
It strikes out again as though gold were clay,
forgetting such El Dorados no map shows,
and even the prospectors who have their day
come to ruin when the ghost towns close.
Yet have no fears. There is a mother lode,
which destiny holds for you in safe-keeping.
Though your heart be weak, mine is bestowed
where only the soul's fierce flames are leaping.
And if in your traveling, you come up empty,
be fueled by my love, your love consenting.

46
THE HAWK

Did you not feel the sweetness of love, my refugee,
under the wild geese heading south or wrapped
in blankets, the world at bay?
      Where were you secretly
hiding while the ring of mountains, snow-capped,
took us in? And we aired our thoughts, careless of
anything but truth, transparent to one another.
What greater gift from those who hover above
than moments warmed by the heart, or the utter
joy when two converge? But absent behind
a wall of pain, in a fog of doubts you wandered.
You were a hooded hawk, unnaturally blind,
and the rare fragrance of our season squandered.
For your heart's habit left you unaware,
and only I, the dreamer, was truly there.

47
EXCUSE

Yes, I know I have not always pleased
or found the center of your natural bent.
You say what's right for me is not the least
ingratiating. You are not content.
Thus do my failures run counter to my will,
which in its blissful ignorance offends,
and in the darkness I feel my way, until
I err, defeating my most cherished ends.
But you would serve the spirit: love and light.
And what is spirit if not generous?
It overlooks the sin or puts it right.
Such frailty is human and innocuous.
Only love's intentions satisfy.
The rest can be amended by and by.

48

MAX

Well, Max, you did your best. And if you turned
your daughter into a son and hid your softer side,
taught her perfection at your workbench,
      and burned
away weakness and tears, yes, it did provide.
Lace and giggles would not have gotten her
      through.
A handsome man in the photographs, you gave
your strength. But from the start she wanted you,
the craftsman, the lady's man she never forgave.
I am one of those — the older men she took apart
to find your love. And if there is something still
not granted, some deep appetite of the heart,
maybe my will will answer where your will
could not. One thing I'll always keep in sight —
you'll want this sweet labor done just right.

49
RETURNING

Absence has no power without the mind,
which has its own long oceans, dark continents too,
or becomes suddenly a sun, and, so inclined,
abolishes the distance in me, in you.
Silence has no power when inner speech
makes a playlet of your starkest fears.
And how am I cast when I cannot reach
you? A nameless stranger shut away from tears.
Doubt has no power. Yet there we must stand
when trust is broken. Then our wisdom fails.
We're blind. And even this gentle reprimand
adds another sickness to whatever ails.
But mind can also mend, expunging blame.
Can love be love which does not do the same?

50
PROOF

Once you said to me my love needs proof.
It is not enough to gaze into your eyes,
or drive eighty miles to be under your roof,
or hold your hand under an autumn sky.
As though this were just some recreation
I'd undertaken. Though geometers
and lawyers engage in such disputation,
there is no certainty argument confers.
The heart is another thing and surely knows,
 — at least if it is not alloyed of tin.
Constancy too neither comes nor goes,
but remembers always its own heroine.
Love cannot be proved, so say the sages,
but look how I labor to set you on these pages.

51

ENLIGHTENMENT

Outside the library I sat in your folding chair.
On the grass you were cross-legged at my feet.
I did not see it then — why you were there —
but went on pontificating in my seat.
Teacher you called me, and you had in mind
those books you read about the ascended masters,
the ones who would lift you and set you free.
    To find
such paragons would undo your life's disasters.
But I was only mortal and could not be
the guru you needed, whose healing love and light
would be unfailing. I had my faults, you see.
And they grew even larger in your sight.
Perhaps the answer is to grow more human,
to love what is, and, by loving illumine.

52

THE TWIN

All the time she was waiting, poised,
that other self, compacted of your pain.
She had a life sometimes in your voice,
and the horror tales that were your sad refrain.
You were not angry. There was no need.
But she was there, waiting for the kill,
the predatory lady who had to feed
on derelict emotions or grow ill.
The smallest thing might become a prod,
something I said or something that I lack.
When the time came for a trip abroad,
the person who went away did not come back.
You I love, but you are not the twin
who left me hanging, twisting in the wind.

FACES

Every man you seek will wear his face,
the horseman who held a loaded rifle at
your back, whose black shirt kept you
      in your place,
who nailed you up in a stalag where you sat.
He used his sex like a weapon to keep you down;
his money was a promise that he never kept.
You lived in the random darkness of his frown
and counted the other women with whom he slept.
You matched his will with a secret ferocity
and wished him dead but learned to bide your time,
became yourself as ruthless, but in this victory
murdered love and, murdering, loved your crime.
The husband that you buried is still alive
and has buried you although you still survive.

54
RATIONALE

How can I love you knowing what I do?
Let's just say your mask came down, and I
saw the beauty to be seen. Or maybe it's true
love obeys no law but its own random sigh.
Or maybe time and place conspire to complete
the thing we are born to, and you were there.
Or an angel, our go-between, had us meet
and watches our fated progress from the air.
Or perhaps you suit me with all your knotty flaws.
Sometimes that happens. Where you are concave,
I'm convex. Life has its inscrutable laws.
Yet all these reasons do not mean a thing.
When love's gong is struck, it can only ring.

55
INTIMACY

Tonight I am feeling the sadness of all the things
you have been through. The stories you allowed me
to know, that you poured out, the shared inklings
of what life has been for you. Evenings when we
lay together there was nothing that you could
not tell me, until I thought I knew you better
than myself. And I felt that my attentions would
make you free, undo every fetter.
I was a caring witness —or so it seemed —
to those events. Of course, it can be a kind of
foolishness to think that people are redeemed
this way, can be healed by the gift of love.
That a lifetime of pain is dissolved, replaced
with something kinder. That nothing goes to waste.

56
A SINGLE WORD

The silence of your displeasure runs so deep
it is like the night sky without a single star.
Or the desolation of a dungeon keep
where a prisoner is sitting without hope
      in the dark.
Should not a beggar with his beggar's bowl
be given a dollop of rice? Or a poor wretch lost
in the sands a thimble of water? Is there no dole
for a homeless child? And all at such little cost?
Lovers unaddressed grow weak with ruin,
unless a soul has pity — what the masters teach.
A simple greeting revives. What's more, a wound
may heal itself within a prayer's reach.
What's given is what comes back.
      Surely you've heard.
So send me in your mercy a single word.

57
SILENCE

You, who outdid Scheherazade, have grown
excommunicatory, withholding the wafer of speech,
no longer spinning tales, silent as a stone,
unlisted number that I no longer reach.
Strange how such distances arise,
where comets can circle close and then depart,
retreating into emptiness, into skies
which chill with endless dark the human heart.
And I who feasted on your every word
now starve. Or rather do contrive these lines,
imaginary conversations that are not heard,
questions without answers, left to my own designs.
But who can say which has the greater power,
silence or language, each which has its hour?

58
THE GIFT

I admit I got a little crazy. I'd drunk
from the fount of your affection and wanted to go
on drinking. In my uncomprehending funk,
I badgered you with words. You who know
Krishnamurti's motto: "I don't mind
what happens." You who stood on a ledge once,
       to die
or find another purchase. So while I complained,
you remained speechless as the sky.
What did I hope for with all my analysis?
You are as you are, and I am overthrown
by the inarticulate realities I miss.
I should have trumped your silence with my own.
But a poet's tongue never will be still.
So take my gift of words for good or ill.

59
MISSING PERSON

This unforeseeable parting, how like a death!
So sudden. And with no appeal. As absolute
as your presence. No farewell or a breath
of sweet solace. All expectations moot.
Not even a morgue to visit. "Yes, that is her.
I know her by her scars, her stiff upper lip."
Missing without a trace. As though you were
some bizarre illusion that had me in its grip.
You who were my sun, my cynosure,
have set. Now in the evening sky I keep
a constellation in your place. It will endure
though graves yawn and grim reapers reap.
Why should I mourn the loss of your affection?
After every death there is a resurrection.

60
THE EXCHANGE

For months my bathrobe hung
       on your bedroom door.
You came that Sunday to drop it off with sundry
other tokens of our love. Like prisoners of war,
stripped of identity, they were exchanged, while we
stood by. You took my silence for disdain.
But I had been a prisoner of yours so long,
I could only bind my wounds and stare. It was pain
kept the screen door between us,
       not sense of wrong.
Love cannot be commanded, and gifts are vain,
no better than the faith that lies behind. This rift
too is futile, since intentions remain.
Let me parse out a paradox to sift:
I was abandoned. That much can be believed.
Yet given is given. Who then is aggrieved?

61
POSTSCRIPT

Even your reappearance after so long
was a strange conundrum. We met four times
that day. The obligatory hug. The singsong
of small talk. The cheerful masks and pantomimes.
We met in a place for soul connections. Here
we began and here came back. The altar remains.
Are we not candles, sometimes lit, my dear,
sometimes out? For love both waxes and wanes.
Avoiding my eyes, you sat opposite
in the class of twelve. Nothing was the same.
When things move on, there is no help for it.
You left me an empty picture frame.
How easy to end when there is no choice.
That night on the telephone — another's voice.

62
MAGIC

I've come to see this love of mine has little
to do with you. My own capacity
it is. I am the stove, you only the kettle.
If there is magic, the magic is in me.
Like a Hollywood set, you were just attached
to fortify illusion. The things I saw in you
were already alive in me. You were a match.
The bonfire was my heart. And how it grew!
Rumi charmed us both with this advice:
When love offers her kisses, you must act.
And only total surrender will suffice,
since what is given always will come back.
Thus have I gained from what I thought I'd lost,
for love goes with me and does not count the cost.

63
LESSONS

What have I learned from you, my dear murshida?
I will not be harmed when I give myself away.
Be watchful. The truly observant eye can read a
world of truth in what tiny things convey.
The spirit does not live in judgment or control.
Intentions, like clouds, are shaped
      and reshaped too.
Feelings become their opposites. Do not console
yourself with affections that are so quickly through.
This one has her story. That one has his own.
Our faces hide a mystery but dimly seen.
God too has a story, but it cannot be known.
So give each his freedom, and do not
      come between.
Take only what is given. And when that is gone,
harvest the meaning — then move on, move on.

64
SCENARIOS

Your silence was the poison I was meant
to take. The gift to shatter the shackles of
desire. And this talon of pain is sent
to tear me that I may know the terror of love.
Not punishment, no. But as a flower
opens to let in the marauding bee,
who comes to plunder in the appointed hour,
for pollen's sake and a new fertility.
This is a kindness you do me, rooting out
indulgence and the pulp of entitlement.
What are these scenarios about,
but the dissolution of disordered intent?
In such a way your curses are kisses too,
and, denied your love, I learn the heart of you.

65
THE AGENT OF AFFINITIES

If not yours, then let me be longing's suitor.
Where you came from there is a world of glory.
The morning air will be my gentle tutor.
And the rose will whisper to me her sweet story.
Though I am banished from your thoughts, I gain
another entrance in the avenues of All.
That is your Source, where I will find you again.
You are a droplet in that waterfall.
Why should I chafe at these austerities?
The anguish of lovers surely is misguided.
Everywhere shines the Agent of Affinities,
and what I found in you is undivided.
I am even richer in my banishment,
since unanswered love is love never spent.

66
MASSAGE

Under Helga's kneading fingers I found the tears
locked in my body, the forgiving words made plain,
as, dancing to music, they came from all the years,
one by one, to bow and be seen again.
A turning reel of lovers, those who drew near,
as close as flesh can get, to beautify
a gesture or make their presence dear,
that I might learn what it is to sigh.
Yet in their gaze I saw what lives in all,
the dross that falls away and what is kept,
even to the end of time, and felt in awe
of the secret beauty that in my nature slept.
What is the harvest that we take above?
I know now love is the harvest, and only love.

67

RENEWAL

The field mouse lives in the eye
      of the red-tailed hawk.
The wandering bee takes the nectar and is gone.
The lover opens his heart, discovers talk
to make sense of blind desire, and goes on.
Today's affection is tomorrow's hate.
This kiss that heals may become a wound.
And yet how can we hope to obviate our fate
when whole worlds blossom and whole worlds
      are pruned?
All is hazard, and yet all is safe.
Feeling in the dark, we become the shape
of what we prove to be. Fruitless, to chafe
at bitter evanescence, which none escape.
Let the field mouse swoon
      in the hawk's sharp talons.
Let the hive grow sweet and mice new skins.

68

THE EMERALD CITIES

My loves too populate those emerald cities,
Jabalqa and Jabarsa, ancient Ozes, aglow
with light, where all the unseen felicities
of the heart can live. Where in a rainbow
lovebirds hover and fly down with a twitter
of greetings to perch on my shoulder.
      Where in reams
of clover my soft bunny learns not to skitter,
and my romping Shelties herd the sheep of dreams.
And you, whom I have embraced, companions on
the way, are addressed in these bright precincts,
a wish apart. For no thing loved is gone
forever, but lives on as light does
      and what light links.
And the Wizard beckons all who are his guests
to join him in endless and unfathomable quests.

NOTES ON SPECIAL WORDS & ALLUSIONS

ishk
The force of cosmic desire that created everything. Divine love.

murshid, murshida
The Sufi word for a spiritual teacher. In the context of the poems this is usually Hazrat Inayat Khan, the presiding spirit at the Abode of the Message, a Sufi community in New Lebanon NY.

Pir
The spiritual leader of a sufi order. While he was alive, The Sufi Order of the West was guided by Pir Vilayat Khan. Its logo is the Winged Heart, the meaning of which is "to rise in love." My education in the intelligence of the heart was guided by Pir Zia Inayat Khan and others who presided over the Suluk Academy, a four-year program in the Sufi way of being.

The Bird Paradise
A bird sanctuary in Petersburg NY, known for its rescue of injured birds of prey.

Shelties
Shetland sheepdogs. Imagine Lassie, only 16 inches high.

Jamshyd
A mythical figure from the ancient Persian epics. He was a poet-king who brought high civilization to his people. Angels and demons buoyed up his throne. He possessed the Cup of Jamshyd, in which he could envision the secrets of the universe. Unfortunately he could not take heaven by storm and was overcome by woman trouble and the forces of darkness. In Fitzgerald's *Rubaiyat of Omar Khayyam* he is mentioned to remind us of transience of glory: "They say the Lion and the Lizard keep / The Courts where Jamshyd

gloried and drank deep." Jamshyd is also the spiritual name of the writer of these sonnets, who hopes to come to a better end.

H. P. Lovecraft
Probably our greatest writer of supernatural horror.

Krishnamurti
A 20th-century spiritual teacher famous for clearing away mental baggage.

Rumi
Thirteenth century author of the Mathnavi and one of the greatest of the Sufi poets. His work is a treasure of observations about the centrality of love. My sonnet sequence is described as an "essay" because it was based on a real love affair exploring the truth of the Sufi message. Like many of Rumi's poems, the sonnets were written in the heat of experience, documenting the various states as they emerged. They constitute the milestones on the journey from human love, with all its disappointments and uncertainties, to the divine love which Rumi wrote about.

Helga
An Austrian masseuse plying her trade in Lanesboro MA.

Jabalqa and Jabarsa
Two cities Sufis say can be visited in dreams or in the imagination, before or after death. They exist in the world of archetypes and make up a spiritual reality beyond time and space.

ABOUT THE POET

I am one of the rays of the Divine Sun. Assumed this body in 1932, in the middle of the Depression, in the cheerful month of June. Endlessly young, like most Geminians, I have always been blessed with a summery life, with lots of time for learning, and running wild in the grassy neighborhoods. (See *Boy From Under the Trees* poems on The Poet's Press website.) Father and mother, decent people, gave me a good foundation. Being a football "hero" in high school got me to Yale. Fell in love with books. Became a teacher. Learned a lot from Alfred Korzybski. Did my doctoral dissertation on the work of Jung. Also fell in love with ten women, five of whom were willing to marry me. *In the Eye of the Red-Tailed Hawk* addresses one who wouldn't. In addition to my wives, I have gotten to enjoy four kids, three grandchildren, two Shelties, three bunnies, thirteen love birds, and two cockatiels. (Learned as much from the animals as from the people.) Studied Joseph Schillinger and started to compose music on the computer. Meanwhile, had time to spend twenty years hanging out with the Sufis. (Jamshyd is my Sufi name.) Did wonders for my spiritual life. Turned me on to Hazrat Inayat Khan and Rumi. Became a Cherag and began presiding at Universal Worship services. All this helped me to learn how to offer wisdom and inspiration in my classes. In my seventies, I am still creating new courses at a small college. Have one on Rumi and two others called Divine Witness and Science & Spirit. Loving every minute. Right now at 77 I am enjoying my twilight years in a kind of monkish solitude and receptivity which gives me plenty of stress-free time to ruminate and be myself. With this kind of energy cooking in me, I radiate blessings on all I meet. If you are still reading this, have some.

www.ingramcontent.com/pod-product-compliance
Lightning Source LLC
Chambersburg PA
CBHW031459040426
42444CB00007B/1145